MARK CUBAN

The Self-made Billionaire Who Rose from Grit to Greatness

CHARLES HERRON

Copyright @ 2024 By Charles Herron

All rights reserved. No part of this book may be reproduced, distributed, or transmitted in any form or by any means, including photocopying, recording, or other electronic or mechanical methods, without the prior written permission of the publisher, except in the case of brief quotations embodied in critical reviews and specific other noncommercial uses permitted by copyright law.

Contents

INTRODUCTION: THE MAVERICK MINDSET

CHAPTER 1: HUMBLE BEGINNINGS

CHAPTER 2: THE HUSTLER'S PATH

CHAPTER 3: FROM COLLEGE TO CORPORATE WORLD

CHAPTER 4: BROADCAST.COM AND THE BILLIONAIRE LEAP

CHAPTER 5: MAVERICKS MASTERMIND

CHAPTER 6: SHARK TANK SUCCESS

CHAPTER 7: BEYOND THE BOARDROOM

CHAPTER 8: CUBAN'S LEADERSHIP STYLE

CHAPTER 9: NAVIGATING CHALLENGES AND CONTROVERSIES

CHAPTER 10: THE FUTURE VISION

CONCLUSION: A LEGACY OF INNOVATION AND TENACITY

INTRODUCTION: THE MAVERICK MINDSET

Mark Cuban is a well-known name in fields other than business. He's not just a millionaire; he's also a leader, an inventor, and, most of all, a man who changed what success means. From working-class roots in Pittsburgh to becoming one of the most influential people in business, sports, and the media, his rise is impressive. Not just Cuba's enormous wealth or business makes him stand out. It's the way he thinks.

Cuba's story isn't about inheriting money or being spoiled. It's about a man who made a lot of money by working hard and being determined to show that anything is possible with the right attitude. From a young age, Mark Cuban had what would become known as the "Maverick mindset": a constant drive for success that didn't follow the norm, didn't accept things as they were, and took risks that most people wouldn't.

He learned early on how important it is to work hard because he grew up in a working-class home. Most kids his age were busy with sports or school, but Cubans were already working hard to save money for basketball shoes. He sold trash bags door-to-door. For him, it was more than just a job; it was his first experience running a business, and it marked the beginning of a lifelong habit of finding opportunities where others did not. His early efforts were frequently small and unknown, but they laid the groundwork for a long and successful career. Early on, Cuban realized that success wasn't about being the best person in the room but outworking everyone else.

Cuban was like any other Indiana University student. He chose the school since it was the most economical option for him, and from the start, he displayed the same drive that would ultimately define his career. He did not only study business; he lived it. When he wasn't in class, Cuban was busy starting little businesses, organizing parties, and learning the ropes of business wherever he could. It wasn't exciting, but each venture was a step forward, another piece of the puzzle that would eventually allow him to think beyond the box in ways others couldn't.

His entrepreneurial path started in his twenties, but his early attempts to enter the corporate world were challenging. After being fired from his first software job for closing a contract without his boss's authorization, Cuban realized that corporate life was not for him. Instead of viewing this as a setback, he saw it as an opportunity to forge his path. His first significant achievement was the establishment of MicroSolutions, a computer consulting firm he founded from scratch. Cuban's hands-on approach and customer-focused philosophy enabled him to rapidly build the business, which he sold for millions of dollars within a few years. This was the first taste of tremendous success, but it wasn't the last.

Cuban's life was drastically changed in the late 1990s when he co-founded Broadcast.com, which revolutionized online streaming. At a period when the internet was still in its infancy, Cuba recognized an opportunity to change how people consumed information. His daring approach paid off handsomely when Yahoo purchased Broadcast.com for $5.7 billion, propelling Cuban to billionaire status virtually instantaneously. But for Cubans, it wasn't all about the money. It was about demonstrating that his unique approach—seeing opportunities where others didn't and taking chances where others wouldn't—could lead to unprecedented success.

Then, in 2000, Cuban made one of his most famous moves: buying the Dallas Mavericks. At the time, the team was struggling both financially and technically. Cuban didn't just acquire the squad; he transformed it by instilling the same enthusiasm, ingenuity, and hands-on leadership that had made him successful in the software industry. Under his ownership, the Mavericks went from losing to winning the NBA championship 2011. Cuban's ownership approach was unlike anything else in professional sports. He wasn't a passive owner; he was on the sidelines, conversing with players and supporters and continuously searching for ways to improve the team's performance. His desire to win and his business savvy helped the Mavericks become one of the NBA's most successful clubs.

However, Cuba's impact did not end with athletics. His debut on *Shark Tank* made him a household figure, as millions witnessed his acute financial understanding and desire to invest in the next wave of entrepreneurs. Cuban was searching for more than immediate success; he wanted innovative concepts and passionate entrepreneurs that reminded him of his early days. His appearance on the show served to solidify his reputation as a straight-talking, no-nonsense investor willing to take enormous risks if he believed in the company's mission.

Beyond his economic undertakings, Cuban is recognized for his honesty and readiness to express his opinions. Cuban never hesitates to share his views, whether on social media, in interviews, or public appearances, frequently sparking debates on politics, business, and technology. He doesn't follow the crowd; he thrives on going against it. This contrarian perspective and his persistent work ethic have propelled him to the pinnacle of success in numerous industries.

His journey demonstrates what it means to be a true entrepreneur. His trip to the top was not smooth or easy, but it was motivated by a genuine conviction that success comes to those ready to work harder, think more significantly, and take risks others would avoid. Cuban did more than develop enterprises; he established a legacy of invention, leadership, and unwavering commitment to greatness.

This book is about more than simply Cuban's financial success; it is also about the attitude that catapulted him to greatness. It requires guts, vision, and a willingness to accept failure as a stepping stone to something greater. Mark Cuban's story demonstrates that anyone can rise from low beginnings to exceptional achievement with enough passion and dedication.

CHAPTER 1: HUMBLE BEGINNINGS

Mark Cuban's journey begins in the bustling city of Pittsburgh, Pennsylvania, known for its rich steel manufacturing heritage and a strong community in its neighborhoods. Cuban was born in a Jewish working-class household on July 31, 1958. His parents were Norton Cuban, an automobile upholsterer, and Shirley, a homemaker. His childhood was modest, with the principles of hard work, ambition, and resilience ingrained from an early age.

Pittsburgh was changing dramatically throughout the 1960s and 1970s. The steel sector was in decline, and many families, including Cubans, were experiencing financial difficulties. Despite their modest finances, Cuban's parents worked hard to provide a supportive home full of love and encouragement. His father frequently worked many jobs to support the family, emphasizing the value of dedication and commitment. This early experience in the workforce taught Cuban that financial security resulted from hard labor and commitment, laying the groundwork for his future endeavors.

From a young age, Cuban had an entrepreneurial spirit that would mold his identity. At 12, he started selling door-to-door waste bags in his neighborhood for money and to save up for a pair of coveted basketball shoes. This experience was meaningful for Cuban; his first introduction to selling and hustling would define his subsequent career. He learned essential lessons about the value of persistence, communication, and the capacity to deal with rejection—skills that will serve him well in today's highly competitive business environment.

Cuban's boyhood was also distinguished by his passion for athletics, notably basketball. Growing up in an area where the sport was famous, he found refuge and thrill on the court. This interest was more than just recreational; it fed his aspirations. He aspired to own an

NBA team in addition to playing professionally. These seemingly distant objectives were based on the conviction that hard work and strategic thought could make dreams a reality. His competitive spirit was sharpened further by numerous hours spent playing pickup games, where he learned the value of teamwork, leadership, and tenacity.

His entrepreneurial tendencies became more pronounced as he approached adolescence. He started several little enterprises selling stamps, coins, and baseball cards. Each enterprise presented a fresh chance for learning, allowing him to understand business dynamics and consumer behavior thoroughly. He rapidly realized that success often depended on finding unmet needs and providing solutions that connected with people. These formative experiences cemented his notion that entrepreneurship was more than just a means of accumulating riches; it was also a means of creating value and having an effect.

Cuban's inventive spirit shone through his high school years at Mount Lebanon High School. He aimed for more than just academic accomplishment; he wanted to combine his knowledge with practical experience. Cuban, known for his charisma and outgoing attitude, organized and promoted student events, demonstrating his marketing and event management skills. His ability to unite people while capitalizing on social trends demonstrated a basic comprehension of commercial fundamentals. These parties were hugely successful, which boosted his confidence and determination to pursue a career in entrepreneurship.

After graduating high school, Cuban enrolled at Indiana University, where he studied business administration. His undergraduate years were significant in his life. At Indiana, he was more than just another student; he was a self-starter who took advantage of every opportunity. He immersed himself in the intellectual and social world, taking on internships and creating numerous entrepreneurial initiatives. He even launched a disco that became the talk of the school, allowing him to combine his passions for music and business while making a good living.

His determination to succeed grew stronger during his time at Indiana. He read books on entrepreneurship and money, gathering knowledge that would be useful in his future endeavors. He surrounded himself with like-minded people who shared his enthusiasm for innovation and business. Networking became essential to his undergraduate experience; he learned to leverage ties with students, instructors, and local business leaders. Cuban realized that the relationships he created could lead to opportunities that formal education alone could not.

Mark Cuban's early years were marked by a relentless work ethic and an entrepreneurial spirit that thrived in adversity. His humble roots in Pittsburgh established a solid basis for his objectives as he traversed the complications of young adulthood. Each difficulty he experienced, whether selling garbage bags or running a college business, ingrained in him the notion that success was possible with hard effort, inventiveness, and a willingness to take risks.

His rise from a working-class household to the halls of academia was defined by a voracious thirst for information and an unwavering pursuit of success. The qualities he learned as a child—hard work, resilience, and a focus on creating opportunities—shaped his personality and business approach. Those early lessons remained at the forefront of his thoughts as he focused on the future, guiding him through business's inevitable ups and downs.

Finally, Mark Cuban's poor beginnings were more than just a backdrop to his success; they were a crucible for the self-made billionaire who became a business and sports powerhouse. His life exemplifies the belief that greatness can come from the most unlikely circumstances and that anyone can achieve their goals with enough determination and creative thought. Lessons learned in his adolescence were only the start of a unique journey, redefining what it meant to be a true entrepreneur.

CHAPTER 2: THE HUSTLER'S PATH

Mark Cuban's entrepreneurial adventure began with the spirit of hustle and tenacity that would shape his life. Growing up in Pittsburgh, Pennsylvania, he was exposed to the blue-collar values of hard labor and resilience. Born into a working-class Jewish family, Cuban learned at a young age that financial security was earned, not given. Norton, his father, toiled diligently as an auto upholsterer, frequently doing numerous jobs to support the family. This early introduction to the importance of a strong work ethic would serve as the foundation for Cuban's entrepreneurial efforts.

He started his first business when he was 12, selling waste bags door to door. He had learned that a local company was paying a hefty commission for selling these bags, so he took advantage of the opportunity. He went door to door in his neighborhood, armed with a few samples and a compelling pitch. It wasn't just a method to generate extra money; it was his first step into the sales world. Each rejection stings, but Cuban quickly realizes the value of persistence. He recognized that every "no" moved him closer to a "yes," and this insight became the foundation of his sales philosophy. The hustle paid off, and he eventually saved enough money to buy the basketball shoes he wanted—his first taste of entrepreneurial success.

Cuban's ventures continued after rubbish bags. Throughout his teenage years, he looked for ways to get money. He sold stamps and coins, searching local businesses and markets for valuable objects to resell. This experience taught him about supply and demand, negotiation skills, and market research. He learned how to detect consumer needs and deliver them competitively. Discovering a rare coin or a sought-after stamp was exhilarating, but the marketing and customer relations lessons were the most valuable.

As he entered high school, Cuban worked several jobs, each of which helped him further his education as an entrepreneur. He worked as a dishwasher at a nearby restaurant, where he learned about the fast-paced nature of the food service industry. This profession taught him the value of teamwork, time management, and the tireless pursuit of customer satisfaction. He recognized every role's importance, no matter how little, and determinedly attacked each assignment. Cuban's work ethic was not overlooked; his employers frequently appreciated his dedication and attitude.

In addition to his restaurant job, Cuban became a barman. This encounter offered him a unique opportunity to improve his interpersonal skills. Behind the bar, he interacted with a broad spectrum of customers and how to discern their moods and preferences. He rapidly learned the intricacies of customer service and the importance of leaving a good impression. Cuban flourished in this milieu, perfecting the capacity to defuse stressful situations and foster a friendly culture. These talents would be helpful in his future business endeavors, as knowing client psychology would be critical to his success.

During his high school years, Cuban's entrepreneurial ambitions grew. He organized parties and social events for his classmates, which were profitable companies. He took on the role of promoter, using his inherent charisma and marketing talents to entice guests. These gatherings supplied him with revenue and allowed him to polish his event-organizing and promotional skills. He learned to generate buzz, engage his audience, and provide a memorable experience. The energy and excitement of the gatherings fuelled his entrepreneurial spirit, boosting his ambition to create and invent.

After graduating high school, Cuban attended Indiana University to seek a business degree. His undergraduate years were momentous, further shaping his business outlook. Cuban was determined to make the most of every opportunity, and his approach to his education reflected this drive. He immersed himself in academics, learning finance, marketing, and management. However, he thrived outside of the classroom.

While in Indiana, Cubans started various businesses, including a small disco that quickly became the most popular spot on campus. This endeavor demonstrated his awareness of industry trends and ability to interact with others. Cuban's ability to create a lively and vibrant atmosphere attracted crowds, and the disco became a financial success. He learned to lead a team, manage logistics, and deliver a memorable brand experience. The disco was more than a business; it was a platform for Cubans to express their creativity and entrepreneurial spirit.

As the disco grew popular, Cubans sought new ways to make money. He became interested in the rapidly growing technology industry, realizing the promise of computers and software. He and a friend started a modest retail business selling computer hardware and software. This venture introduced him to the world of technology, and its potential immediately took him to creativity and disruption. Cuban learned the subtleties of inventory management, marketing strategy, and customer service in a fast-changing industry. This early exposure to technology would pave the way for his future endeavors, as he recognized that adaptability and foresight were required for success.

Throughout these encounters, Cuban gained a firm trust in his abilities to create and invent. He knew that business was more than just making money; it was about solving issues and adding value to people. Each obstacle he faced, whether managing a crowded bar, planning a party, or running a retail store, fuelled his desire and taught him crucial lessons. Cuban developed a mindset that saw setbacks as chances for progress, which served him well throughout his career.

Mark Cuban's early career as a hustler was defined by unwavering persistence and a desire to learn. Each venture, from selling waste bags to opening a disco, increased his understanding of business principles. Cuban's ability to see possibilities, react to hurdles, and cultivate customer relationships defined his business trajectory.

As he matured, the lessons he learned along the way shaped his identity as a businessman and visionary. Mark Cuban's experiences as a hustler established the groundwork for his subsequent success, demonstrating that the path to greatness is frequently forged through hard effort, inventiveness, and an uncompromising devotion to achieving one's goals. His narrative is a compelling reminder that with enough effort and resourcefulness, anyone can carve their own road to success, regardless of where they begin.

CHAPTER 3: FROM COLLEGE TO CORPORATE WORLD

Mark Cuban's transfer from college to the corporate world was a watershed moment, laying the groundwork for his eventual success as a technology entrepreneur and millionaire. After earning a degree in Business Administration from Indiana University in 1981, he was passionate and driven to establish a name for himself in business. The talents he had developed via his previous companies and the principles he had learned in college would help him negotiate the competitive terrain of corporate America.

As Cubans entered the workforce in the early 1980s, the technology industry began to take shape. The digital revolution was on the horizon, and there were plenty of opportunities for those prepared to take chances and embrace innovation. With a degree and an unwavering business mentality, Cuban sought positions allowing him to apply his skills and earn crucial experience.

His first crucial corporate involvement occurred in 1982 when he joined a software company called Your Business Software. As the company's first sales agent, Cuban was in charge of marketing PC software, a novel notion at the time. This position allowed him to immerse himself in the rapidly evolving world of technology, where he quickly realized the enormous growth potential. He embraced the work fiercely, aiming to create an impression and outperform sales targets.

Cuban's innate charisma and awareness of client demands helped him succeed in this capacity. He refined his sales talents by learning to identify potential clients' problems and propose remedies via the software products he was selling. During this period, he was also acutely aware of the rapid developments in the technological industry. He took it upon himself to stay current on developing trends and inventions, which would become one of his hallmarks. This desire to learn and adapt distinguished him from his colleagues and paved the way for his future success.

He left Your Business Software in 1983 to work for MicroSolutions, which provided computer consulting and networking solutions. His responsibilities increased as he assumed a more strategic position. He used his sales experience and technical understanding to assist firms in optimizing their operations with technology. This employment allowed him to delve deeper into computers and networking, which aided his knowledge of how technology may change industries.

At MicroSolutions, Cuban's entrepreneurial inclinations began to bloom. He realized that many small firms were trying to integrate technology into their operations, frequently needing more means and ability to do so successfully. This observation generated an idea: he could start a company that provided comprehensive technology solutions suited to the specific needs of small and medium-sized businesses. His objective was to make technology accessible and beneficial to companies of all sizes, which reflected his entrepreneurial career.

After years of hard work and effort, Cuban co-founded MicroSolutions, and his drive to provide high-quality service soon paid off. Under his guidance, the company saw tremendous growth, producing significant revenue and building an excellent reputation. Cuban's ability to create outstanding client relationships became critical to MicroSolutions' success. He recognized the importance of trust and communication in developing long-term relationships and made it his top mission to ensure that every customer felt appreciated and supported.

After several successful years at MicroSolutions, Cuban took the risk of selling the company to CompuServe for $6 million in 1990. This sale was an essential milestone in his career, giving him the financial means and freedom to seek new opportunities. Cuban's time at MicroSolutions I provided him with vital insights into the technology industry and the abilities required to handle the complexity of firm ownership and corporate structure.

With the wind at his back, Cuban embarked on the next stage of his entrepreneurial journey. He began looking at investing opportunities in technological businesses, motivated by his enthusiasm for innovation and desire to keep ahead of developing trends. He was particularly interested in the Internet's potential to revolutionize business and information access. Cuban's strong eye for opportunity and willingness to take risks made him a forward-thinking investor in a changing market.

Cuban made a massive jump into digital media in 1995 when he co-founded Broadcast.com with his friend and fellow entrepreneur Todd Wagner. The startup was founded to transmit audio information over the Internet, a revolutionary concept that soon acquired popularity. Cuban's sales experience and technical knowledge were critical to Broadcast.com's growth. He was not only concerned with the technical side of the business but also with how to market it properly to attract users and advertise.

Under Cuban's guidance, Broadcast.com thrived, becoming a pioneer in internet streaming services. Investors and consumers were drawn to the company's creative strategy and commitment to offering high-quality content. Cuban's adaptability to the quickly changing digital landscape exemplified his innovative attitude. He saw the opportunity for expansion in the Internet media field and took advantage of it, establishing Broadcast.com as an industry leader.

Broadcast.com was bought by Yahoo! for an incredible $5.7 billion in stock in 1999, barely four years after its inception. This enormous transaction propelled Cuban into the realm of billionaires and cemented his reputation as a significant figure in the technology industry. Broadcast.com's success resulted from years of hard work, determination, and a constant pursuit of innovation. Cuban's transition from academia to the business world was marked by his willingness to take risks, adopt new technology, and form significant relationships—characteristics defining his career.

Reflecting on this period, it is clear that Cuban's collegiate experiences and early corporate employment established the groundwork for his future endeavors. His time at Indiana University gave him the theoretical understanding required to comprehend business principles, while his work in technology businesses gave him practical skills and insights. Cuban's ability to harness his education and expertise enabled him to confidently and successfully negotiate the complexity of the technology sector.

Cuban's journey from corporate to entrepreneur is an example for aspiring business leaders. His journey demonstrates the value of hard effort, adaptation, and the courage to embrace chances when they arrive. The skills and experiences he learned during this early stage of his career shaped his approach to business in the following years, propelling him to unimaginable heights as a self-made millionaire and household figure in entrepreneurship.

CHAPTER 4: BROADCAST.COM AND THE BILLIONAIRE LEAP

In the fast-changing landscape of the mid-1990s, the InternetInternet was emerging as a revolutionary medium, and Mark Cuban was eager to capitalize on its promise. Cuban was ready for his next enterprise after successfully selling MicroSolutions and building a sizable financial cushion. He co-founded Broadcast.com with his friend Todd Wagner in 1995, and the company quickly became synonymous with internet streaming.

Broadcast.com was founded on a simple but powerful idea: to enable live streaming of audio material over the InternetInternet. Cuban and Wagner recognized that as more people acquired access to the InternetInternet, demand for online content would skyrocket. They envisioned a platform that could broadcast live radio and music, allowing people to listen to audio broadcasts from anywhere in the world. This vision was ahead of its time, as many people were still getting used to the concept of the InternetInternet itself.

His entrepreneurial spirit and technological acumen influenced the company's trajectory. He recognized that the platform must provide a seamless, high-quality streaming experience to attract customers. To achieve this, Cuban invested in cutting-edge technology and infrastructure, guaranteeing that Broadcast.com could manage high traffic levels without sacrificing performance.

Cuban and Wagner worked relentlessly to form agreements with radio stations, music labels, and content producers to create a diverse audio library. This focus on variety distinguished Broadcast.com from its competitors. While other companies specialized in static web pages or rudimentary audio streaming, Broadcast.com provided a comprehensive solution that allowed customers to listen to live broadcasts, music playlists, and even sports events in real-time.

His sales experience proved essential as he began to promote Broadcast.com. He was skilled at presenting the platform to prospective clients, demonstrating how live streaming might increase their reach and engagement. Cuban organized marketing efforts highlighting the platform's potential, leveraging his industry connections to increase adoption. His unwavering excitement and persuasive abilities drew attention, allowing Broadcast.com to acquire traction in a growing market.

In 1998, the company took a crucial step forward when it was granted a patent for its technology, which enabled audio and video streaming via the InternetInternet. This patent cemented Broadcast.com's reputation as an industry leader and supplied a valuable asset that would later be critical in discussions with possible owners.

As the dot-com boom progressed, Broadcast.com drew the attention of investors and tech titans alike. Cuban recognized that the time was right to pursue acquisition prospects. In early 1999, he began conversations with Yahoo!, a rapidly developing internet portal looking to extend its products in the digital media arena. Cuban's vision precisely fit Yahoo!'s objectives, making a solid argument for a merger.

After months of discussions, Yahoo announced its acquisition of Broadcast.com in April 1999 for a stunning $5.7 billion in stock. The acquisition was one of the largest in internet history, propelling Cuba to billionaire status virtually instantaneously. This enormous sale demonstrated the worth of Broadcast.com's revolutionary technology and marked a watershed moment in the growth of digital media.

Following the acquisition, Cuban became a household name known for his money and innovative approach to technology. The sale of Broadcast.com elevated him to a prominent player in the technology industry, giving him the resources and visibility he needed to explore other enterprises and investments. With his newfound money,

Cuban expanded his interests by investing in various startups and enterprises that shared his love for innovation.

Cuban's success with Broadcast.com established him as a sought-after expert and analyst in the technology business. He began appearing on television, discussing entrepreneurship, investing methods, and the future of technology. His outspoken style and forthright thoughts won over audiences, and he quickly established himself as a regular on business news programs and talk shows.

Furthermore, Broadcast.com's significance extended beyond financial success, representing a paradigm shift in media consumption. The platform paved the path for mainstream streaming services such as Spotify, Apple Music, and Netflix. Cuban's insight into recognizing the potential of online streaming has far-reaching consequences, permanently altering how consumers access and consume media material.

As Cuban reflected on his experience with Broadcast.com, he realized the value of adaptability and innovation in an ever-changing environment. The company's success was not just due to timing; it resulted from hard labor, strategic thought, and a steadfast commitment to pushing boundaries. Cuban's experience with Broadcast.com was a model for other entrepreneurs trying to impact the tech sector.

Following the sale, Cuban pursued new challenges and opportunities, motivated by a passion to create and inspire others. The lessons he learned at Broadcast.com were the foundation for his future endeavors, including owning the NBA's Dallas Mavericks and involvement in several humanitarian activities. His narrative shows the power of vision, perseverance, and the unwavering pursuit of success in the rapidly changing world of technology.

CHAPTER 5: MAVERICKS MASTERMIND

In 2000, Mark Cuban made a critical choice that would cement his name in sports: he bought the Dallas Mavericks, a floundering NBA organization. The acquisition occurred when the Mavericks' reputation was tarnished by a lack of postseason success and a shrinking fan base. However, Cuban saw opportunities where others saw difficulties and was determined to turn the squad into a powerhouse.

Cuban's foray into professional basketball was more than owning a franchise; it culminated in his lifetime interest in sports and competition. He had always been a passionate basketball fan, and owning the Mavericks allowed him to combine his business skills with his passion for the game. The purchase was not without controversy, with many questioning whether a digital entrepreneur could effectively manage a sports organization. Cuban remained undeterred, eager to bring his new ideas and business energy to the Mavericks.

One of his first actions as owner was restructuring the team's management and operations. Cuban recognized that a great team requires more than required on-court skills; it must also have a strong foundation in coaching, scouting, and player development. He recruited Donnie Nelson as general manager and quickly began spending on players on and off the court. His hands-on approach to team management included attending games, meeting with players, and communicating directly with fans, which was unusual among NBA owners.

Cuban's desire to invest in technology and analytics helped the Mavericks stand out from their rivals. He used complex statistical analysis to assess player performance and identify future talent, a strategy that was novel at the time and gave the Mavericks a competitive advantage. The squad began to incorporate data-driven decision-making into its recruitment process, allowing it to find undervalued athletes with considerable potential.

He made a risky move in 2001 when he drafted Dirk Nowitzki, a young German power forward who went on to become one of the NBA's finest players. Cuban's foresight in choosing Nowitzki was a game-changer for the organization. With Cuban's backing, Nowitzki grew into a superstar, and the Mavericks swiftly became a dominant force in the league. Cuban's dedication to developing talent and building a great team culture aided the Mavericks' success under Nowitzki's leadership.

However, Cuba's ownership model had obstacles. He was noted for his passionate and even provocative presence in the arena. His boisterous behavior frequently generated headlines, such as shouting at referees and interacting with fans. While some praised his passion, others accused him of being overly boisterous and distracting from the game. Nonetheless, Cuban's unwavering dedication to the Mavericks' success won him over the Dallas community, and his efforts to interact with fans improved the team's image.

The Dallas Mavericks made their first appearance in the NBA Finals in 2006. Cuban's vision and unwavering determination had paid off, and Dallas was thrilled. The club played the Miami Heat, headed by superstars Dwyane Wade and Shaquille O'Neal. The series was dramatic, with the Mavericks leading 2-0, but they eventually fell in six games. Despite the tragedy, Cuban remained positive and determined to assemble a championship-caliber club.

The Mavericks remained competitive in subsequent years but firmly established themselves in the 2010-2011 season. Cuban had made clever moves, recruiting veteran players like Jason Kidd and Tyson Chandler to complement Nowitzki's scoring ability. The Mavericks went into the playoffs with a fresh sense of purpose and determination. Cuban's faith in his squad and willingness to invest in their success fostered a culture of perseverance and confidence.

The Mavericks faced various hurdles during the playoffs, including a complex series against the defending champion Los Angeles Lakers. However, Cuban's leadership and the team's determination carried them forward. The Mavericks again advanced to the NBA Finals, meeting the Miami Heat in a rematch. Following their recent defeat, the Mavericks attacked the series with focus and purpose.

The Finals were a rollercoaster of emotions, with the Mavericks facing early challenges. Despite this, the squad rallied, thanks to Nowitzki's outstanding performances. In a dramatic Game 6, the Mavericks won the championship with a 105-95 victory, their first NBA title. Cuban's pleasure was evident as he celebrated with his teammates on the court, tears running down his cheeks.

His victory was more than just a personal success; it also marked an important event in Dallas's sports history. He had taken the Mavericks from perennial underdogs to

NBA champions, and his inventive management approach had established a new standard for how sports teams should function. The victory resonated well with the Dallas community, uniting fans and fostering pride in the city.

Cuban's journey with the Mavericks continued after the title, as he stayed committed to improving the team and fan experience. His commitment to philanthropy and community service cemented his reputation as a revered figure in Dallas. The Mavericks' success under Cuban ownership demonstrated the power of vision, ingenuity, and determination to achieve greatness on and off the court.

In the years after, Cubans have continued to embrace difficulties and seek new possibilities in the NBA and beyond. The lessons he learned while with the Mavericks demonstrated his belief in the value of tenacity, adaptation, and the unwavering pursuit of excellence. Throughout it all, Cuban remained loyal to his team, inspiring generations of basketball fans and entrepreneurs alike.

CHAPTER 6: SHARK TANK SUCCESS

Mark Cuban rose to prominence in venture capitalism in 2009 when he joined the cast of *Shark Tank*, a reality television show in which entrepreneurs pitch their business ideas to a panel of wealthy investors known as "sharks" in the hopes of getting investment. This move was not only aeer turn for Cubans but Cuban sanded moment for the show, as his lively personality and abundance of experience appealed to spectators and budding entrepreneurs.

His appearance on *Shark Tank* came when entrepreneurship was gaining popularity in the United States. The economic collapse of the late 2000s prompted many people to explore alternate paths to financial stability, and Cuba became a source of encouragement for those willing to take the risk. He brought to the show his financial resources and a solid understanding of what it takes to start and run a successful firm. His unique perspective as a self-made billionaire elevated the show's legitimacy, enticing viewers eager to learn from his accomplishments and faults.

Cuban demonstrated a personable and direct style on the *Shark Tank* stage. Unlike some other investors, who may be more quiet or calculated, Cuban was recognized for his honesty and eagerness to urge entrepreneurs to think critically about their projects. He frequently asked probing questions about the contestants' business ideas, market strategies, and long-term goals. His questioning approach was intended to elicit honest reactions, allowing him to assess the viability of the business idea and the entrepreneurs' passion and devotion to it.

His impact on Shark Tank went far beyond simply negotiating deals. He became a mentor and sounding board for other contestants; for example, during a pitch for a business named DoorBot, which later became Ring, Cuban invested and provided suggestions on the product's marketing and design. He recognized the potential of the unique home security gadget and saw an opportunity to use his network to help the firm develop. This hands-on approach yielded a profitable investment and highlighted Cuban's dedication to supporting innovation and entrepreneurship.

Cuban's ability to spot trends and invest in new countries was crucial to his success on the show. He had a talent for identifying promise before it became popular. For example, when he invested in Snagajob, a platform that connects hourly workers with employers, he recognized the changing nature of the labor market and the growing desire for flexible employment options. Cuba's vision in these instances enabled him to make profitable investments and influence industry trends.

His eagerness to share his experiences and lessons learned from his entrepreneurial career won over both contenders and viewers. He frequently shared stories from his history, such as when he sold garbage bags door-to-door as a kid to raise money for basketball tickets or his early problems with Broadcast.com. These examples taught resilience, tenacity, and the value of learning from mistakes. Cuban's sincerity and relatability elevated him beyond the status of an investor, making him a role model for aspiring entrepreneurs.

He also used *Shark Tank* to debunk widespread misconceptions about venture finance. He emphasized that investment is more than money; it is a partnership. He frequently stated that a successful investor should be a resource for entrepreneurs, providing advice and support as they overcome the hurdles of running a business. His approach inspired many finalists to see investment as more than just a financial transaction but a collaborative effort to create something meaningful together.

Cuban's participation in Shark Tank has impacted not only the specific firms he has invested in but also the overall entrepreneurial scene. His participation has motivated many people to pursue their entrepreneurial goals, promoting an environment of innovation and creativity. Many prospective entrepreneurs have been inspired to take risks and create their businesses after seeing Cubans engage with participants, negotiate deals, and offer support.

His role as an investor on the show evolved throughout the seasons. He became well-known for his concentration on technology-driven businesses, frequently favoring ideas that took advantage of developing technologies. This tendency was notably evident in his investments in firms such as LuminAid, which provides solar-powered lighting for disaster assistance, and Eco-Warrior Princess, a sustainable apparel line. Cuban recognized that the future of business lay in sustainability and technology, and he actively sought out entrepreneurs who shared his vision.

Beyond the boardroom, Cuban appeared on *Shark Tank* to advocate for social reform and community engagement. He constantly emphasized the significance of giving back, encouraging entrepreneurs to explore how their firms may benefit society. This approach resonated with many participants, prompting them to consider their corporate social responsibility and how they could use their businesses to improve the world.

Cuban's influence on *Shark Tank* and the business ecosystem continues to expand. He has established himself as a trusted person in the investment world, advocating for small firms and promoting entrepreneurial education through his platform. Through efforts such as the Mark Cuban Foundation and active participation in mentoring programs, he stays devoted to inspiring the next generation of entrepreneurs. His appearance on *Shark Tank* not only improved the show but also left a lasting impression on the corporate world.

Mark Cuban's experience on *Shark Tank* has changed how people think about entrepreneurship and investment. His sincere desire to help others succeed and his acute financial skills have made him a key player in the entrepreneurial environment. By investing in creative ideas and cultivating the aspirations of young entrepreneurs, Cuban has built a lucrative portfolio and fostered a culture of risk-taking and innovation. During his tenure on *Shark Tank* Mark Cuban demonstrated that success is determined not only by financial gain but also by the impact one can have on others' lives.

CHAPTER 7: BEYOND THE BOARDROOM

Mark Cuban's influence extends far beyond the confines of his Dallas Mavericks headquarters and the set of *Shark Tank*. As a visionary entrepreneur, investor, and philanthropist, his contributions to numerous industries, such as technology, media, and sports, reflect a diversified career marked by a commitment to innovation and social responsibility. Cuba's ventures reflect his economic skill and conviction in giving back to society and fostering the next generation of thinkers and doers.

Cuban's investment style is distinguished by a keen sense of opportunity and a readiness to embrace emerging technology. Beyond his high-profile investments on Shark Tank, he has built a broad portfolio of health tech, entertainment, and e-commerce firms. For example, Cuba invested in NantHealth, a health-tech business that leverages technology to improve patient care and outcomes. His interest in the healthcare sector originates from his understanding of the industry's potential for innovation and ability to substantially impact people's lives.

In the media scene, Cuban has established himself as an influential player. Following the sale of Broadcast.com to Yahoo, he pursued new prospects in digital media. He founded the HDNet network and renamed AXS TV, a channel focused on live entertainment and music content. This enterprise displayed his dedication to significant material and awareness of the changing media world. AXS TV became well-known for its live concerts, celebrity interviews, and original programming, demonstrating Cuban's commitment to giving people unique experiences.

Cuban's approach to media goes beyond just entertaining. He has continually emphasized the necessity of independent and diverse voices in the industry. His involvement in *The Broadcast*, a platform for local news stations to share stories and coverage, illustrates this dedication. By encouraging local media outlets to connect with their communities, Cuban hopes to promote journalism and ensure that essential stories reach the public, bucking the tendency of centralized media control.

Philanthropy is another critical component of a Cuban's life, in which his riches serve a purpose other than personal benefit. He has participated in a variety of humanitarian efforts, with a focus on education, health care, and disaster assistance. One example is his support for *Cuban's Kids*, a program providing educational tools and opportunities to disadvantaged Dallas youngsters. This effort strives to close the access gap to high-quality education by providing scholarships, mentorship, and career development programs to assist young people reach their full potential.

His philanthropic initiatives also include disaster relief. Following the destruction wrought by Hurricane Harvey in 2017, he vowed to donate $1 million to help rebuild

Houston and support local organizations that help affected families. His prompt response demonstrated his confidence in the power of communal resilience and togetherness during times of distress. Cuban's philanthropy ideology is based on the belief that those who have the means owe it to others to help them, and he urges other wealthy persons to follow suit.

In addition to his charity endeavors, Cuban's influence in sports extends beyond his ownership of the Dallas Mavericks—he is an outspoken supporter of player rights and mental health awareness in the NBA. Cuban has frequently spoken out about the need to help athletes beyond their on-court success, emphasizing the need for tools that address the mental health issues that players face. His dedication to creating an environment prioritizing well-being has struck a chord with many in the league and the larger sports community.

Cuban's advocacy includes social issues. He has been a vocal supporter of LGBTQ+ rights, promoting diversity in his business and personal life. This position has won him over admirers and established a precedent in the sports world, where discussions about diversity and representation have gained traction. Using his platform to raise awareness and promote equality, Cuban has established himself as a leader in the battle for social justice.

Furthermore, his involvement in the technology industry is not just as an investor but also as an innovator. Cuban has been active in various technology projects, including his work in the Bitcoin industry. As a proponent of blockchain technology, he has invested in several cryptocurrencies and decentralized financial firms, demonstrating his trust in technology's revolutionary power. Cuba has regularly emphasized the significance of adopting digital currencies and its propensity to disrupt established banking systems, urging businesses to seize the opportunities in this fast-changing market.

His active social media usage further demonstrates Cuban's influence as a thought leader. He is recognized for his open conversations on platforms like Twitter, where he discusses business, technology, and current events. His direct connection with his audience has enabled him to connect with various followers, sparking discussions beyond business and into more significant societal issues. Cuban uses his platform to promote his businesses and urge conversation and action on pressing issues.

As an author and speaker, Cuban has shared his experiences and knowledge with people all over the world. His publications, including How to Win at the Sport of Business, teach essential lessons based on his personal experiences, emphasizing the value of hard effort, tenacity, and a willingness to take risks. Through his speaking engagements, he inspires aspiring entrepreneurs and seasoned business leaders to pursue their passions and question traditional wisdom.

Mark Cuban's legacy is defined by his constant pursuit of innovation and dedication to making a positive difference in society. Beyond the boardroom, he personifies the values of entrepreneurship, generosity, and social responsibility. Whether investing in new technology, campaigning for social justice, or empowering future generations via education, Cuban's achievements extend beyond the business world, making an indelible effect on various industries and communities. His path serves as a reminder that success is defined not just by financial achievements but also by the positive improvements one can make in the world.

CHAPTER 8: CUBAN'S LEADERSHIP STYLE

Mark Cuban's leadership style is as dynamic and diverse as his entrepreneurial path. Cuban, known for his bravery, inventiveness, and unusual approach to business, has established himself as a transformative leader who pushes people around him to think differently and push the boundaries. His leadership philosophy is based on sincerity, unshakeable devotion to quality, and a desire to inspire creativity.

One of the distinguishing features of Cuban leadership style is his willingness to take risks. He frequently emphasizes that fear of failure should not prevent people from pursuing their goals. Cuban's own experiences, particularly the launch of Broadcast.com, support this perspective. When he co-founded Broadcast.com in the late 1990s, the internet was still a relatively new technology, and many people were skeptical about the sustainability of streaming audio and video online. However, Cubans saw opportunity, whereas others saw uncertainty. His decision to take that leap of faith paid off and established him as a technological pioneer. This bravery connects with his team and coworkers, inspiring them to take risks and think outside the box.

Cuban leadership emphasizes innovation. He actively seeks out fresh ideas and fosters a culture of innovation in his organizations. Cubans know the need for adaptation in a continually changing market. He has created an environment where team members feel empowered to suggest new ideas, try unconventional techniques, and challenge the status quo. This inventive approach is evident in how he manages the Dallas Mavericks, where he has used cutting-edge technologies, including virtual reality and advanced analytics, to improve the fan experience and boost team performance.

His leadership style is open communication and transparency. He promotes open communication and encourages his people to express their thoughts, regardless of their position within the organization. This strategy encourages trust and collaboration, creating an environment where team members feel appreciated and heard. Cuban's honest communication approach extends to his social media contacts, where he provides ideas and connects with his followers authentically. This directness increases his leadership presence and sets the tone for his teams to follow in their interactions.

Cuban's unique leadership style is shown in his adherence to a flat organizational structure. He feels that hierarchy can limit innovation and collaboration. By reducing the number of bureaucratic levels, Cuban enables his team to take ownership of their jobs and make decisions on their own. This strategy speeds up decision-making and instills a sense of responsibility in team members. Cuban's hands-on leadership approach keeps him involved in the day-to-day operations of his enterprises, allowing him to stay connected to his teams and create strong connections with employees.

Furthermore, Cubans strongly emphasize culture and values in their organizations. He realizes how influential a positive corporate culture is in attracting and retaining talent. Cuban encourages a quality and complex work culture, with each team member expected to give their all. He also values diversity and inclusiveness, believing that varied perspectives contribute to better problem-solving and innovation. Cuban's dedication to these ideals is evident in the Mavericks' hiring policies, as he aggressively searches out applicants with diverse backgrounds and experiences, building an inclusive atmosphere that represents the community they serve.

Cuban politicians are also known for their strong sense of social responsibility. He believes that successful leaders are obligated to give back to their communities. This belief is evident in his philanthropic endeavors, which include actively seeking methods to promote educational programs, health care, and social justice projects. Cuban encourages his staff to participate in community service and donate to causes they care about, reinforcing that leadership goes beyond the office.

Another component of Cuban's leadership style is his ability to adapt to changing circumstances. The business landscape continuously changes, and Cuban understands the need to pivot and alter strategy as needed. He loves change and encourages his team to do the same, instilling a mindset that sees obstacles as chances for progress. This agility was evident in his response to the COVID-19 epidemic when he immediately developed safety measures for the Mavericks and assisted nearby businesses and communities during unparalleled uncertainty.

A tireless pursuit of knowledge also distinguishes Cuban's leadership style. He is an avid reader who seeks fresh information through books, podcasts, or conversations with thought leaders. Cuban encourages his team to have a similar mindset, emphasizing the value of constant learning and development. This dedication to personal and professional development fosters a culture of curiosity, motivating people to broaden their skill sets and keep current with industry trends.

Mark Cuban's leadership style is characterized by daring, inventiveness, and a strong desire to promote an inclusive and collaborative atmosphere. His approach fosters risk-taking, embraces change, and emphasizes the significance of values and culture in organizations. As a leader, he drives corporate success and motivates others to think critically, act decisively, and make meaningful contributions to society. Cuban's legacy as a revolutionary leader inspires aspiring entrepreneurs and seasoned professionals, serving as a role model for anyone seeking to make their mark in business.

CHAPTER 9: NAVIGATING CHALLENGES AND CONTROVERSIES

Mark Cuban's path to success has been challenging. He has faced numerous hurdles and conflicts that have challenged his resolve, resourcefulness, and leadership talents. From his early entrepreneurial endeavors to his public persona, Cuban has overcome several challenges, making him the influential figure he is today.

He began his entrepreneurial journey as a teenager, selling waste bags door-to-door for additional cash. This early hustle paved the way for his subsequent commercial undertakings. However, the path to success was challenging. After launching Broadcast.com with his friend Todd Wagner, the two-faced the growing difficulties many companies faced. They had to raise funds, handle market instability, and deal with the pressures of competition in a fast-changing tech sector. Cubans' persistence and resourcefulness helped them overcome these obstacles. He frequently focuses on the lessons he learned during these formative years, emphasizing the value of perseverance and adaptation in the face of adversity.

After selling Broadcast.com to Yahoo for $5.7 billion in 1999, Cuban became one of the wealthiest people in America almost overnight. However, the acquisition coincided with the iconic dot-com bubble crash, which resulted in a dramatic drop in tech stocks and many layoffs. Some criticized Cuban, believing he took advantage of market conditions to cash out at the high. He remained unfazed, arguing that the sale was a strategic choice based on the company's development prospects. Despite the complaints, the bubble's aftermath was harrowing for many entrepreneurs. Cubans saw firsthand how fast fortunes could shift in the technology business. Rather than letting the slump define him, he saw it as an opportunity to refocus and diversify his investments. He ventured into sports, entertainment, and other economic enterprises, including purchasing the Dallas Mavericks in 2000, which proved to be a watershed moment in his professional career.

Fans and observers were skeptical of Cuban's acquisition of the Dallas Mavericks. Many questioned his ability to oversee an NBA organization effectively. His boisterous and opinionated demeanor sparked early controversy, particularly in his dealings with referees and league officials. On the other hand, Cuban accepted the challenge and committed to changing the team's culture. The Mavericks had several obstacles during his ownership, including player performance, management issues, and budgetary limits. Cuba's unique leadership style conflicts with traditional basketball operations. His desire to disrupt the established quo drew both praise and condemnation. For example, he introduced novel procedures, such as using technology to analyze player performance, which was unusual then. This forward-thinking strategy helped the team succeed but also caused debate, with some viewing it as a break from traditional sports franchise management approaches.

One of the most significant difficulties came in the 2011 NBA Finals when the Mavericks played the Miami Heat, led by superstars LeBron James, Dwyane Wade, and Chris Bosh. Cuban came under considerable media pressure, with many predicting a quick defeat for his club. However, Cuban's faith in his players was rewarded when the Mavericks won the title, marking a watershed event in team history. This triumph cemented his place in the sporting world and demonstrated his ability to handle high-pressure situations.

Cuban's career as an NBA owner was not without controversy, particularly over the Mavericks' internal culture. In 2017, the organization was accused of workplace wrongdoing, prompting a thorough inquiry by the NBA. Cuban was thrown into the spotlight as the owner, drawing criticism for handling the situation. Critics questioned if he had created a hostile work atmosphere, and many believed he should take more responsibility for the franchise's culture. Cuban responded by openly acknowledging the need for change and taking urgent action. He hired outside consultants to conduct an extensive examination before implementing new policies to encourage diversity and inclusion. Cuban's honesty throughout the process highlighted his dedication to responsibility. He not only took steps to address internal difficulties, but he also actively participated in conversations regarding workplace culture in sports. This encounter was a watershed moment for Cuban, demonstrating his capacity to tackle complex challenges head-on and accept responsibility for his decisions.

His openness has also made him a divisive character in the public sphere. He is known for his strong comments on various matters, including politics, economics, and the NBA's current status. This eagerness to speak his opinion has elicited both praise and criticism. During the COVID-19 pandemic in 2020, Cubans' views on economic relief for businesses and the role of government received a lot of attention. His recommendations for dealing with the crisis demonstrated the complexity of leadership in times of uncertainty. While some commended his aggressive approach, others accused him of being overly ambitious or unrealistic. Cuban's reactions to public scrutiny demonstrate his resilience. Rather than fleeing from the spotlight, he continued to campaign for topics he believed in, using his position to raise awareness and effect change.

Cuban's activities outside of basketball also encountered difficulties. As an investor on the reality TV show *Shark Tank* He has met several startups asking for finance. While his investments have frequently produced big profits, he has also encountered obstacles due to the competitive nature of the startup industry. Cuban has declined numerous pitches, and some entrepreneurs have publicly chastised him for his actions. However, he believes being direct and honest is crucial in the investment industry. His direct approach to appraising enterprises has garnered him both acclaim and criticism from entrepreneurs and spectators.

Furthermore, Cuba's involvement in technology has presented difficulties in reacting to quickly changing market conditions. He has dealt with problems such as regulatory monitoring and changing customer tastes. For example, his investment in the bitcoin industry has elicited enthusiasm and skepticism. Cuban has been vocal about his trust in blockchain technology's promise but has faced criticism for investing in a volatile market. His capacity to adapt and grow in the face of such problems demonstrates his entrepreneurial spirit and willingness to take risks.

Mark Cuban's journey through adversity and controversy demonstrates his tenacity and dedication to growth. Rather than avoiding obstacles, he has confronted them, learning valuable lessons. His ability to negotiate public scrutiny, address worker difficulties, and adjust to changing market conditions has cemented his status as a visionary leader. Cuban's tale demonstrates the value of accountability, honesty, and perseverance in reaching success, encouraging other people to face their obstacles and strive for greatness.

CHAPTER 10: THE FUTURE VISION

Mark Cuban's outlook on the future is profound and complex, informed by his experiences as a successful entrepreneur, investor, and media figure. With years of experience navigating the fast-paced worlds of technology and business, Cuban presents a vision reflecting optimism and a clear sense of the challenges ahead.

Cuban, a pioneer in the technology business, particularly with his pioneering startup Broadcast.com, has always had his finger on the pulse of innovation. He believes that advances in artificial intelligence (AI), machine learning, and data analytics will significantly impact the future of technology. Cuban believes that new tools will not only improve business processes but will also substantially alter customer interactions. He frequently emphasizes the need to use AI to create personalized experiences, suggesting that organizations embracing this trend will succeed, while those who reject change will stay caught up. According to him, the next generation of successful businesses will be those who use technology to increase productivity and understand and anticipate consumer requirements.

Cubans are also well aware of the ethical consequences of these breakthroughs. He frequently stresses the need for a framework to enable responsible technology use, emphasizing the need for transparency and honesty in business. As he envisions a future in which AI plays a vital role, he asks that corporations address any biases in algorithms and protect user data. He calls for policies that keep businesses accountable, urging a balance between innovation and ethical responsibility. This strategy represents his business habits and serves as a model for others in the industry.

Furthermore, Cuban's vision for the future includes education. He supports better educational reform for a technologically driven economy to educate the next generation. Cuban argues that traditional educational systems frequently need to allow students to negotiate the challenges of modern business contexts. He pushes for a curriculum focus critical thinking, problem-solving technological skills like coding and digital literacy. He encourages young people to take risks and express their ideas by encouraging entrepreneurship as a realistic professional route. Cuban has also invested in various educational initiatives, believing that access to high-quality education can enable people to become innovators.

Cuban's business strategy emphasizes adaptability and resilience. He recognizes that the terrain constantly changes, and successful businesses must be willing to pivot and learn from mistakes. Cuban frequently discusses his setbacks and the lessons he learned from them, emphasizing that failure is merely a stepping stone to tremendous success. He encourages ambitious company leaders to keep a growth attitude, stressing that the ability to adapt and innovate in the face of adversities is critical for long-term success.

Social responsibility is another important aspect of Cuban's vision for the future. He believes that firms must actively tackle societal challenges, including inequality and environmental sustainability. Cuban's philanthropy efforts reflect his desire to have a good impact, as he invests in initiatives that promote education, healthcare, and community development. He envisions a future in which businesses are judged not only on their financial performance but also on their contributions to society. Businesses that prioritize social good, he believes, will not only improve their reputations but will also attract more loyal customers and motivated employees.

Regarding his legacy, Cuban wishes to be recognized as a trailblazer who pushed others to think large and take chances. He wants to be remembered as someone who not only succeeded but also promoted the values of innovation, creativity, and ethical responsibility. Cuban frequently discusses the value of mentorship and knowledge sharing to inspire the next generation of entrepreneurs to pursue their objectives without fear. He understands that his influence extends beyond his businesses to the motivation he gives to young inventors.

Mark Cuban's vision for the future combines technical optimism, social responsibility, and a dedication to education and mentoring. He envisions a world where innovation drives progress, and corporations play an important role in creating a better society. Cuban's investments, advocacy, and personal example inspire others to embrace change, think critically, and make a big difference in their communities. His legacy as an entrepreneur and creator will impact future generations, inspiring them to manage the difficulties of a quickly changing environment with creativity and purpose.

CONCLUSION: A LEGACY OF INNOVATION AND TENACITY

Reflecting on Mark Cuban's life and work reveals that his journey exemplifies the power of vision, resilience, and invention. Cuban exhibits an entrepreneurial spirit, having grown from humble beginnings in Pittsburgh to become a self-made millionaire and an essential person in the business and entertainment industries. His unwavering pursuit of achievement is characterized by a willingness to take chances, learn from mistakes, and adapt to changing circumstances.

Cuban's success story is not only about his wealth but also about his impact on others. His role as an investor on *Shark Tank* has changed the game for young entrepreneurs, giving them financing and essential advice. By championing creative ideas and encouraging young company leaders, he has created an entrepreneurial culture that motivates people to pursue their passions and believe in themselves.

Furthermore, Cuban's commitment to social responsibility demonstrates a larger sense of what it means to be successful. He understands that success includes money gain and the potential to make a meaningful societal difference. Through his philanthropic activities and advocacy for ethical corporate practices, he sets a strong example for others in the sector, urging them to think about the ramifications of their work beyond earnings. Cuban's vision of a future in which firms prioritize societal impact reflects a rising recognition that long-term prosperity requires a commitment to the greater good.

As he looks to the future, Cuban's perspectives on technology and education provide a road map for navigating an increasingly complex environment. His campaign for educational reform emphasizes the importance of educating future generations about the demands of a technologically driven economy. He promotes critical thinking and innovation, fostering a culture where young minds can thrive and contribute to society's progress.

Mark Cuban's legacy is defined by his entrepreneurial accomplishments and enormous impact on the corporate world. He exemplifies the belief that success is more than just amassing cash; it is about making a difference and leaving a lasting impression. His journey encourages us to take on difficulties, pursue our passions, and strive for perfection while acknowledging our responsibilities to others. As we reflect on his life, we are reminded that the actual measure of success is how we help people around us and contribute to the betterment of society. Mark Cuban's tale is a compelling reminder that we can all impact the world with vision, determination, and a commitment to invention.

www.ingramcontent.com/pod-product-compliance
Lightning Source LLC
Chambersburg PA
CBHW070359230526
45471CB00006B/2637